VIA Folios 101

STONE WALLS

Gil Fagiani

BORDIGHERA PRESS

Library of Congress Control Number: 2014944623

ARTWORK: Jim Pignetti

"100 Proof"

© 2014 by Gil Fagiani

All rights reserved. Parts of this book may be reprinted only by written permission from the author, and may not be reproduced for publication in book, magazine, or electronic media of any kind, except for purposes of literary reviews by critics.

Printed in the United States.

Published by
BORDIGHERA PRESS
John D. Calandra Italian American Institute
25 West 43rd Street, 17th Floor
New York, NY 10036

VIA FOLIOS 101
ISBN 978-1-59954-078-8

OTHER BOOKS BY GIL FAGIANI

Crossing 116th Street, Skidrow Penthouse (2004)
Rooks, Rain Mountain Press (2007)
Grandpa's Wine, Poets Wear Prada (2008)
A Blanquito in El Barrio, Rain Mountain Press (2009)
Chianti in Connecticut, Bordighera Press (2010)
Serfs of Psychiatry, Finishing Line Press (2012)
Logos, Guernica Editions (2015)

ACKNOWLEDGEMENTS

An earlier version of "The *Scapular* Medal" was published in *Wired Hearts* Spring, 2003.

"Chippies," *The Italian American Community News,* Volume 14, Number 11, 2006.

"Green Onions," *Performance Poets Literary Review,* Volume 10, 2006.

An earlier version of "The Cinder Block Wall" was published in *Italian Heart and American Soul,* Edited by Ed Maruggi, Winston Publishing, 2004.

An earlier version of "Murray the K's Holiday Revue" was published in *Rooks*, Rain Mountain Press, 2007.

"Surprise Party," *Möbius: The Poetry Magazine,* Volume 28, 2010.

"No Glove," *Mudfish,"* 2011.

"Firstborn," *Philadelphia Poets, Volume 18,* 2012.

"Drip Drop by Dion," *First Literary Review—East,* November 2013.

"The Weeds," *Newtown Literary,* 2013.

"I Meet Dad High on Heroin," *Boog City,* Issue 81, 2013.

"Shadowboxing," "Factory Job, 1969," *Voices in Italian Americana,* Volume 25, Number 1, 2014.

"Shame," *First Literary Review—East,* pending November 2014.

"Bughouse Birthday," *New York City Voices,* Spring/Summer 2013.

"Duck and Cover," *First Literary Review—East,* September 2013.

"The Freak," *Paterson Literary Review,* pending 2015.

"Nativity Scene," *Built with Faith: Place Making and the Religious Imagination in Italian New York,* Edited by Joseph Sciorra, University of Tennessee Press, forthcoming, 2015.

To my father, Mario Matthew Fagiani

Never raise your hand to your kids. It leaves your groin unprotected.

Red Buttons

CONTENTS

1   Firstborn

SURPRISE PARTY

5   *Duck and cover!*
6   Bill and Fred's
7   Eggnog
9   Nativity Scene
11   "So Rare" by Jimmy Dorsey
12   Second Grade
13   Kiddie Rides
14   Surprise Party
16   Disillusion
17   Buck O'Brien
19   "Don't Let Go" by Roy Hamilton
20   How I Didn't Learn to Play the Trumpet

NO GLOVE

25   Rock Wars
26   James
29   "We Belong Together" by Robert & Johnny
30   A Dog Named Dickie
32   The Weeds
34   Paper Route
35   Dad Meets *Mister Roberts*
36   No Glove
38   Tender Meanie
39   Rubber
41   The Phil Jones Dance Studio

SHADOWBOXING

45   Shadowboxing

TURNED AROUND

49   In Praise of Frogs
50   Cold-Blooded
51   The Spaghetti Benders
53   "Green Onions"
54   Business
56   Hollywood Scars
57   Turned Around
58   *War of the Worlds*
60   We Were Friends
61   Sidekick
62   The Awakening

CARS

67   The Scapular Metal
68   Why Dad Loved Louis Armstrong
69   At Sixteen
70   High School Motorhead
71   Super Sport, 1963
73   Suburban Article of Faith, 1961
74   The Freak
77   Motorhead's Wardrobe
78   . . . *the way I feel tonight* Roy Orbison
79   Class Struggle in the Connecticut Countryside

STONE WALLS

83   Dad was a businessman
84   Stone Walls

85	Guider's Field
87	"Hello Stranger" By Barbara Lewis
88	Shame
89	Hanging Out with Richie
91	Murray the K's 1964 Holiday Revue
92	Race Relations
94	"Drip Drop" by Dion
95	Factory Job, 1969
96	I Meet Dad High on Heroin
97	Bughouse Birthday
99	Admissions
100	The Refusenik
102	The New Jacket
103	Doo Wop Ornithology
104	The Cinder Block Wall
106	Chippies

MUSICAL SOURCES

109	ABOUT THE AUTHOR

Firstborn

male, to boot.
I start life in the Bronx
Italian neighborhood,
Villa Avenue.
Mom loves me so.
Aunts and uncles adore me.
Grandma cherishes me,
shows me off everywhere.
The butcher dotes on me
so do the fruit vendor,
the shoemaker, the tailor.

They love me in *siciliano,*
napolitano, abruzzese,
Bronx-ese, broken English.
They plump me up
on mozzarella, meatballs,
lasagna, *torrone,*
almond cookies.
They stroke my hair,
pinch my cheeks,
slip me silver dollars.

When I'm five, my parents
move to Connecticut.
Nobody's crazy about me there.

Surprise Party

DUCK AND COVER!

1950-52

Girls and boys crouch
under desks
backs to windows
—walls of death—
eyes shut tightly
hands covering faces
faces buried in arms
fearing for their pets
under the mushroom cloud
wear dog tags
with a melting point
of 1400 degrees.

BILL AND FRED'S

I squeeze behind the glass counter, pick
Candy Buttons—the challenge of biting off
the dots without eating the paper.
Atomic Fireballs—spicy cinnamon jawbreakers—
who can suck them the longest?
Candy Cigarettes—chalky sugar sticks
daubed in red food coloring—let's spook Mom!
Bonomo's Turkish Taffy—shatter it into a zillion
pieces, a single bar lasts through a double feature.
Wack-O-Wax Lips, Wack-O-Wax Fangs,
cherry-flavored gum; play now, chew later.

EGGNOG

Mom fries them
boils them
poaches them
scrambles them
(with milk,
without milk)
makes frittatas
with virgin olive oil
bacon bits
mozzarella
salami,
but I won't bite.

Friday evening
when Dad's paesans
come by
for their weekly poker game
mom drops an egg
in a silver cocktail shaker
adds milk
sugar
a drop of vanilla
and shakes 'til frothy.

Mr. Calamia's
kinky chest hair
crawls out
of his undershirt.
He turns to me.

Drink your eggnog, kid;
it'll put lead in your pencil.
Mom blushes.
Dad pours a beer
foam rising
my lips never touch the cup.

NATIVITY SCENE

Always the dandy, with pearl
cufflinks, cat's-eye pinky ring,
he never had a callus on his hand,
Dad boasted about his father,
whose brilliant schemes
Dad brought to life without protest.

The sculptured umbrella trees
in front of the two-family house
at 3312 Rochambeau Avenue,
the backyard rose garden,
with fountain, flamingos,
lily pond brimming with goldfish,
the basement bar with brass spittoons
—all Dad's handiwork—
where grandpa recounted his rise
from immigrant *poveraccio*
to prosperous clothing designer.

Above all, the Nativity scene:
six feet of painted plaster hills,
a rivulet of running water,
the blinking star of Bethlehem,
the imported figurines of angels,
shepherds, Three Kings, Holy Family,
the birth of *Gesù Bambino,* which grandpa
narrated every Christmas Eve before
a hushed audience of family and *paesani.*

But it was here in the Bronx,
after Dad bought a home in Connecticut,
where grandpa did bend his back,
adding to the Nativity scene:
plastic buffaloes, lasso-throwing
cowboys, Indians on horseback,
and, for shrubbery, green Hawaiian leis.

"SO RARE" BY JIMMY DORSEY

Fog rolls out of a crocodile's mouth
along a stagnant river

A carousel filled with yelping puppies

A litter of kittens feeding on
the phosphorescent guts of a dead pigeon

The salty spray of braking water skiers

SECOND GRADE

I sit in the back of Miss Bruno's class.
Don't know anyone, don't hear a word
she's saying. My stomach hurts.

She starts asking kids questions.
I twitch and keep my head down.
Suddenly I'm seized by an urge to scream.

The urge grows stronger. I fight hard
to drive it out of my head. But the more I try,
the stronger it grows until, before I know it,

I'm shouting: *Ahaaaah!* Kids laugh; Miss Bruno
stares at me, *What's wrong, Gilbert?*
Nothing, I mumble. After class she says:

*Your behavior is unacceptable I won't
tolerate yelling in class.* I remember her
sour breath, her phlegmy voice, the hair

snaking out of her nostrils, a black
stump in the bottom row of her teeth.
I never screamed again.

KIDDIE RIDES

On the ground, broken leg,
swarm of yellow jackets.

Under the bedspread,
crab claws, piranha jaws.

On the bowl, bloody hands
behind the shower curtain.

SURPRISE PARTY

Mom asked what kind of pie
I would like for my seventh birthday.
Blueberry, I said, and off I flew,
past the culvert that brought the brook
from under the street into my backyard,
past the stone wall marking the end of the road,
until I reached the fir and elm trees,
and smelled the odor of skunk cabbage.

Reaching the basin of the brook,
I surveyed the box turtles,
as still as the rocks they rested on,
the yellow heads of the leopard frogs,
the nest of baby black snakes.
A prince among my peers,
I spoke to them for hours,
using a dead sapling as my microphone.

I went home for dinner,
opened the front door.
Surprise! Happy Birthday!
I jumped back
like I'd stepped on a bee's nest.
Seated around a purple pie
were friends and classmates.

I shrank from them,
slipped out the back door
to the brook bed in the backyard,

fleeing through the culvert's mouth,
spider webs clinging to my face,
dampness swallowing me,
the echo of Mom's voice
no longer reaching my princedom.

DISILLUSION

Howdy Doody Show, 1957

Hey, kids, what time is it?
The Peanut Gallery roars:

It's Howdy Doody time!
Commercial break. Buffalo

Bob sucks on a cig. Ushers
bark, *Shut up, you friggin' brats!*

BUCK O'BRIEN

I was king of the cut-ups in third grade
—Miss Harrison tied me up with jump rope
when I wouldn't sit still. You were the bruiser,

first pick for all the teams. Day of Little
League tryouts, you fired a fastball into my ribs.
I hit the ground, struck out four times.

At Woodway Country Club, I watched
you play hockey, when a puck you clipped
flew up a bank and struck me in the head.

I almost beat you, hooked a pickerel
the length of a baseball bat. My line broke.
You walked off with the biggest fish.

When I asked for ten cents to buy candy,
you gave me a Mercury Head dime worth 65 bucks.
I put it in my pocket when your back was turned.

The fall of '59, I lifted weights, confidence rising,
invited you to my house to work out.
Showed you bent-over rowing, French curls.

You lifted a barbell without tightening a clamp.
The plates slid off, clattering onto the floor.
Before leaving, you pinned me to the ground,

knees digging into my forearms,
dribbling spit up and down like a yo-yo,
while I turned my face, closed my eyes.

"DON'T LET GO" BY ROY HAMILTON

Cattle scurry up the ramp
of the meatpacking plant

A train shutters to a stop
in a cloud of lemon mist

Nipples like cavatelli
drip tomato sauce

HOW I DIDN'T LEARN TO PLAY THE TRUMPET

Uncle Bepe grew up so poor, he smoked
cigarette butts picked up from the street,
which is how he figured he caught TB.
When he gave me his trumpet, he said
he quit playing while convalescing
in a sanitarium.

I had already managed to get a sound
out of Dad's army bugle,
and, urged on by Mom, agreed
to take free trumpet lessons
with my third-grade music teacher,
Mr. Thrailkill, who, lacking a single hair
on his head, kids called Chrome Dome.

Born with strong lips and lungs,
and the ability to quickly grasp
the melody of a piece of music,
I was a natural on the horn.
After six months, Mr. Thrailkill,
sensing my inborn talent,
referred me to study
with a classically-trained tutor.

I played lead trumpet in my junior high
and high school bands and won
a scholarship to Juilliard School of Music.
While attending classes I rented
a cheap apartment in East Harlem.

*It was in my uptown neighborhood
that I fell under the spell of Tata
Guerrero, a recent immigrant
from Cuba, who taught me
the rudiments of Afro-Cuban music.*

*When I began to jam with some
of New York City's best Latin bands,
I quit Juilliard and formed my own group.
The girls loved my sound, followed
wherever I played, dubbing me "Golden Gil."
I used to joke I had to hire a man
with a club to beat them off me.
After a feature story in the New York Times
I began to get bookings in the most prestigious
venues in the world: Paris, London, Tokyo.*

I stayed after school on Thursdays—
my favorite day because *The Lone Ranger*
appeared on TV Thursday evenings—
and Mr. Thrailkill gave me musical lessons
in a musky room with two other boys,
one studying the ukulele, the other the tuba.
I was learning to play "Home on the Range"
when Chrome Dome went out on sick leave
without a replacement, Mom mumbled about
private lessons, Dad groused about rising expenses;
I joined the Rock and Mineral Club,
Uncle Bepe's trumpet finding a dusty home
in an attic crawl space.

No Glove

ROCK WARS

Springdale, Connecticut, 1952

I'd just made friends in the neighborhood
when I got caught up in the endless rock wars.
I fought under the command of Henry Holt
against Butchie Malissimo and his Bambinos.
Rumbled alongside Henry in the turf brawls
with Ned Cochran and his Crew Cut Crazies.

I took my bruises, shoulder whacks, leg lumps.
Had my head wrapped in gauze, arm in a sling,
body streaked in Mercurochrome.
But the memory that cuts deepest was a skirmish
with strangers on Sterling Place. Henry didn't
know them—so he ordered their annihilation.

We seized the high ground alongside a bluestone
driveway. I dodged a rock rainfall, then wound up
and threw a four-finger-wide stone, watching it
arch upward, then slowly descend, bouncing off
the head of someone whose face I never saw,
but in later years could never stop wondering
how badly I hurt him—my nameless
childhood enemy.

JAMES

You had an egghead look
like your schoolteacher dad:
honeydew haircut, round shoulders,
lens-magnified eyes,
rhubarb-colored frames.

You plied his pedantry,
bethought it boorish
to give pets names
and called your half-Doberman,
half-dachshund: *Dog*.

Maintaining Dog's
inborn intractability,
you grinned,
ordered Dog to *Kneel!*
She grew stiff,
stared at your boots,
wagged her tail.

You dug rock 'n' roll
but only owned one 45,
"Rumble," by Link Ray
and the Raymen,
that you played
until the mournful menace
of its guitar chords
drove me from your room.

You told me you perused
your sister's diary
to study her sex life
but held out from jerking your gherkin
for fear of shooting blood.

You led Dog and me
behind the wooden schoolhouse
where a new brick addition
was being built, leaned a board
against a wall, shouted at Dog: *Kneel!*
and shimmied up.
Dog barked, tried to follow,
but her paws couldn't grip the wood.

From below, I could see you
rummaging through cans.
I yelled that I wanted to come up,
but you rained down scraps of wood,
electrical cable, bent nails.

Hearing a whistle, I stepped aside,
just as a cement bucket
zoomed by my shoulder
and hit Dog in the center of his back,
flattening him like roadkill.

You said you had miscalculated,
only meant to keep us at bay
so you could have unfettered
first dibs on the goodies
the workmen left behind.

At the burial in your backyard,
you played "Rumble,"
hollered: *Kneel!*
and lowered Dog,
with frayed packing cord,
into the ground.

"WE BELONG TOGETHER" BY ROBERT & JOHNNY

I stand in a black '57
Impala convertible

At an intersection, I smell lilacs
and honeysuckle

On one shoulder, a cardinal;
on the other, an indigo bunting

A DOG NAMED DICKIE

The only dogless kid in Springdale,
I bugged Dad till he brought home Dickie,
a beagle who came with papers attesting to his pedigree.
Dickie's old master lived in Brooklyn
and let him go: a beagle,
with its oversensitive olfactory organs,
can go stir crazy locked up all day.
I swore to Dad I'd feed Dickie,
bathe him, brush his teeth, take him out
twice a day to do his doodie.

Dickie balked at domestic life,
ran off our quarter-acre plot.
It seemed just when Dad's train arrived—
before he could sit down for supper—
he would be tramping through woods
tracking down Dickie.

Fidgety—Dad said it was his pure breeding—
if Dickie wasn't let out when a scent seized his sniffer
he'd get the Hershey squirts, brown down a rug,
puke on a blanket, run up and down the stairs.
I should have cleaned him up
but it always seemed Mom
got the soap and water before I could.

I loved Dickie, always meant to take care of him.
After dad gave him away to an upstate farmer,
I carried his photo in my pocket until it fell out

while I was hopping on stones in a marsh
collecting pollywogs.

THE WEEDS

Last of the old-time Yankees,
the Weeds never mixed
with their suburban neighbors
and kids said the younger brother was psycho,
pulling a knife on trick-or-treaters
when they knocked on the door.

A fence thick with vines and branches
blocked a view of their yard,
vibrant with snorts, grunts, moos,
clucking, cawing. I once spotted
the elder Weed driving his pick-up truck
with a live deer in the front seat.

When the peacocks came,
their piercing cries echoed
through the neighborhood
He-lp! He-lp! He-lp!
At first, thinking someone needed a hand,
I ran down and rattled the gate door,
but the younger Weed waved an ax
and scared me away.

I got used to the peacocks' cries,
saw them parading on the sidewalk
by the Weeds house,
their upright purple plumes,
the rainbow eye
of their erect tail feathers.

One day a police car stopped
and two cops asked about reports
of a man shooting at pet dogs,
when the peacocks cried
He-lp! He-lp! He-lp!
What's that? the cops asked.
Sounds like somebody's in trouble, I said,
pointing to the Weeds house.

When the cops arrived,
the younger Weed cursed at them,
shotgun in hand
and, after a brief standoff,
he was taken away in handcuffs
—to the funny farm, I heard—
and never seen again.

PAPER ROUTE

I could never keep track
of what people owed me
and after a week's work
I was lucky to break even.

In those days, people
disciplined their dogs
by whacking them
with rolled-up newspapers.

No wonder the mutts
growled and did their best
to bite me—I was
their master's arms supplier.

One customer said, *You'll find
your money where you throw
the paper; throw it in the bush,
you'll find your money there.*

DAD MEETS *MISTER ROBERTS*

How did Dad feel when he saw *Mister Roberts?*
Henry Fonda plays the executive officer on a cargo ship.
Tired of his dull duties, he wants more than anything
to be transferred to see combat before the war ends.

Dad grows bored with his cavalry unit,
a bunch of rich kids raised on horseback.
All they do is parade up and down
the Main Streets of America.

In *Mister Roberts,* Captain Morton blocks
Fonda's repeated requests for a transfer.
He knows Fonda's warm relationship with the crew
is key to his pristine record supplying the US fleet.

Dad signs a list posted by his first sergeant
for men who want a transfer to a new unit.
Later crosses his name off when a friend
alerts him the signees will be shipped to the front.

Mister Roberts finally gets transferred to Okinawa,
where he is killed in a Japanese kamikaze attack.
When the war ends, Dad takes advantage
of the GI Bill, buys a Cape Cod in the suburbs.

NO GLOVE

Although a paperboy,
I didn't have money
to buy a baseball glove
because Dad squirreled away
my earnings in a college fund.

He used to preach how
you either make money
with your brain or your back,
and he decided
I'd make mine with my brain.

So I stole a glove from the candy store,
reached behind the glass display case
where I used to pinch penny candy,
and stuffed a first baseman's glove
—the only kind they had—
into my paper sack.

Next morning I showed up
at the pickup baseball game,
where the boys
played their hearts out
and the girls cheered them on.

I rated a "C" as a batter
but "F" as a fielder
and nobody ever chose me.
That day, Butchie —the Homerun

King—Malissimo
needed a second baseman,
and when he saw my new glove,
picked me for his team.

The fingers of my mitt
were stiff and blunt as wood paddles,
and when I tried to scoop up
an easy grounder,
the ball glanced off my glove,
and the runner made it to second base.

The girls booed.
More balls rolled my way,
but they never landed
in my glove pocket;
I bobbled grounder after grounder.

The bases were loaded
and, in a squeeze play,
the shortstop threw the ball
underhand to me. It bounced
off the side of my glove.
My teammates joined the girls
chanting: *Retard! Retard!*
Butchie tossed me off the field.

That's when I returned to frog hunting.
At least I could score a few laughs
releasing croackers in the girls' coat room.

TENDER MEANIE

Piano practice, Mozart score,
you ate cornflakes

before Little League games,
told guinea-wop jokes,

saved me from drowning
at Boy Scout camp

RUBBER

In seventh grade I won second prize
in my junior high school science fair
for a project titled *Water:*
People's Slave, People's Master.
Dad had become an expert on H_2O
after Hurricane Diane almost washed
our house away in 1955.

He built three life-like plaster models:
a desert, a forest, a swamp, to show
the differences in their water tables.
I tried to add a tree here, a bush there,
a bit of lettering,
but he pushed my hand away—
his high standards couldn't tolerate
my 12-year old dabbling.

In eighth grade I submitted
to my school science fair
a project titled *The Many*
Valuable Properties of Rubber.
Dad built an exhibit showing
how rubber—both natural and synthetic—
is processed from trees and chemicals
and is made into a finished product
by calendering, extrusion, or molding.

My sole contribution was to carry
the project into my junior high school gym

and place it on the shiny wood floor.
It didn't win a prize but caused
a sensation when, on the evening
the judges determined the winners,
one of my classmates draped a condom
over my nameplate.

THE PHIL JONES DANCE STUDIO

No fear, like the fear of asking a girl to dance,
at The Phil Jones Dance Studio. The press referred

to him as the local Gene Kelly, his dancers
appeared on the Ed Sullivan Show four times.

A wounded vet, he'd show you up for slacking
by sitting down and taking off his wooden leg.

SHADOWBOXING

SHADOWBOXING

Hook to the ribs:	Being a lousy student.
Right jab:	Not joining a team sport.
Kidney shot:	Defying Dad.
Hammer fist:	No girlfriends in high school
Haymaker:	Messing with heroin.
Sucker punch:	Marrying my ex.
Overhand right:	Delaying my social work career.
Rabbit punch:	Working too long at the crazy house.
Roundhouse:	Being a lush.
Left uppercut:	Not going to Italy until my forties.

Turned Around

IN PRAISE OF FROGS

I love the skin of frogs
so creamy to the touch
so pleasurable in the hand.

I love their bulging eyes
marble-shaped, unmoving
that take in everything.

I love their sinewy thighs
how they spring from sunlight
to the pond's muddy bottom.

I love their long tongues
how they furl out
and roll up a juicy bug.

I love the twang of bullfrogs
vibrating in the lush
heat of an August night.

I love frogs in mating season
how their eggs float on water
like rafts of tapioca.

I love their spring peeping,
a shout-out to life
its perpetual renewal.

COLD-BLOODED

I watched in horror as Mr. Baxter,
glasses gleaming in the sun,
shifted his big traveling salesman's
belly forward
as he brought a hoe down,
severing a garter snake in two.

A teenage crusader
for serpent's rights,
I'd stayed the hand
of my own father earlier
in the week when, building a stone wall,
he'd wanted to drop a boulder
on a nest of black snakes.

At the sight of two
black and yellow squiggles,
I raved about snakes being
man's friend, killer of rats, bugs,
trying all the while to pull the hoe
out of Mr. Baxter's hand
until it slipped through my fingers,
smashing his glasses in his face.

After his second operation,
I was made to see a family counselor,
who suggested I perhaps lashed
my lizard too much, and a priest,
who reminded me that snakes
symbolize man's evil side.

THE SPAGHETTI-BENDERS

In school it seemed the Eye-
talians were the bottom bunch,
It was the wopsters who fought
and couldn't be taught,
the wopettes who painted their mugs,
had sewer mouths and names
that never ended: Rosaria Romanelli,
Raffaela Scognamiglio.

When I lay my lamps on the frightened
farm girl just arrived from Kentucky,
I leaped at the chance to shine the slime light
on somebody with less status
than the spaghetti-benders.

She had scaly skin,
broom-bristle hair,
and wore velvet-rot togs.
I dubbed her *Scabby*
a name my Yankee sidekick
Freddy-Boy Mueller, assured me
would be my claim to fame
since, no sooner had I uttered it
than it rolled through the ranks
of Dolan Junior High School:
Scabby in the hall
Scabby in the mall
Scabby every place she went
and in case a private moment

put her at ease, Freddy-Boy and I
took turns telephoning her at home
SCABEE! SCABEE! SCABEE!

Her parents overheard one phone call
and forced her to cough up our names.
They visited Freddy Boy's folks,
wearing their barnyard best,
and pleaded with them to stop their son
from calling their daughter *Scabby*.

Freddy's white bean parents
humphed and hollered and asked
why they didn't stop by my house
and they answered that they were scared
'cause they heard Eye-talians
were touchy, had long knives,
short fuses.

"GREEN ONIONS"

I'm fourteen, and it's a slow,
leaf-burning day in October
at the annual Danbury Fair.
I hear the electric beat
and slip away from my parents,
past wooden poultry cages,
stalls of sleepy cows and sheep,
long tables of squash, beans, cauliflower.

Through the dust and smoke
of the merry-go-round,
the Caterpillar, the bumper cars,
I see three fortyish blondes
on a wooden platform
in silver sequined bathing suits
grinding to the guitar
of Booker T.'s "Green Onions."

The woman in the middle
has dark flaps of flesh
hanging under her arms.
Below the stomach pouches
of the others, stray pubic hairs
jut out like black beetle legs.
I bolt from the tent,
guitar licks lashing me
like a cat-o'-nine-tails.

BUSINESS

Saturday Kiddie Matinee features:
Abbott and Costello Meet Frankenstein.
Accustomed to their antics—the fast talk,
the clownish pranks, the dopey puns—
we expect a few laughs and monster lite.

When Frankenstein appears,
he isn't a caricature, but hulking
and horrible—like the original,
and Count Dracula and the Wolf Man
are the real things, played
by Lon Chaney and Bela Lugosi.

Freddy and I fidget, cringe,
let loose a snicker here and there,
but Jerry's face goes ghostly,
he rears up, arms twitching,
mouth open, unable to utter a sound.

Next day Jerry's mom goes rabid
on us: Jerry couldn't sleep,
nightmares all night, *you're both older,
should know better; he's banned
from the State Theater!*
To make sure he doesn't sneak in,
she cuts off his weekly allowance.

Saturday comes and Freddy devises
a plan to get money so Jerry

can join us to see *Werewolf*
in a Girls Dormitory.
We pool old books we've read
and knock on neighbors' doors
claiming to be selling books to raise
money for our school's PTA.

Things are going swell, we just need
a quarter more, when Mr. DeLuca
opens the door. A holier-than-thou-type,
his son's about to become a priest.
What fundraiser? I'm a PTA member,
do your parents know about this?

He calls our parents. Jerry can't
leave his yard for a month,
Freddy's tell him to stay away
from Mr. DeLuca, and Dad—
a businessman who hopes
my entrepreneurial spirit
has been awakened—advises
that, as a future salesman
I should know my customers better
and emphasize that all profits
are going into my college fund.

HOLLYWOOD SCARS

A hailstorm of candy
whips through the air:
Raisinetes, Goobers,
Jujubeans, I'm used to it;
besides, it just stings a little
unless some dodo pitches
a Tootsie Pop or all-day sucker.
I hunker down,
feed my face—I'm no fool—
keep my eyes glued
to the marvels on the screen.
Kids can throw stuff
until their arms fall off
for all I care. That is until
the day I notice two rips
in the big screen
—some punks hurled
rocks or bolts—
one rip like a ragged circle;
the other, a wavy teardrop.
It's not so bad when images
on the screen are light,
but Daffy Duck looks
like he's been shredded
by shotgun pellets,
Mighty Joe Young's face
plagued by jungle rot,
and patches of Jane Russell's
bathing suit
eaten away by acid burns.

TURNED AROUND

More often we sat turned around
to watch the show, back rows filled
with hoods, their black jackets open,
greasy pompadours splashed across
pimply faces, and dolls with beehive
hairdos and sweaters that stretched over
what looked like sets of steel funnels.
The hoods might slug a jug
of Thunderbird, light up a Lucky,
clean their nails with a switchblade.

Best of all was when they made out,
guys groping, girls groaning.
Once I saw a bare breast
illuminated by an usher's flashlight
another time, a fight broke out
over whose doll was whose,
cops called after the manager's
face was scratched, arm bitten.
Freddy claimed he saw a couple
slide to the floor and do it on a bed
of candy boxes and buttered popcorn.

WAR OF THE WORLDS

The news blazed in our eyes
like the tail of a comet.
It's all we thought about,
all we dreamed about.
When we woke up, our lips
were moving: *War of the Worlds*
will be at the State Theater
this weekend.

Everyone stayed on their best behavior
except me, I messed up, came home
after the Fire Department's whistle
shrieked my 8 P.M. curfew.
I was always late, and Dad roared :
You're restricted to our property
for the weekend!

At first I didn't believe it,
although I knew compared
to other kids' fathers,
Dad stood out as the strictest,
with his Old World rules,
Freddy called him *Mussolini*.
But surely he would relent,
give me another warning;
anyone would agree forbidding me
to see *War of the Worlds*
was too far out, too over the top,
too vicious, cruel, deranged.

I moped around; mute, mad,
depressed, Dad wouldn't budge.
In desperation I begged Mom,
—like the Blessed Mother
with the Almighty Father—
to use her charms, intercede, plead
with my old man to lighten up,
have mercy, and let me join every
single kid in the neighborhood
and make the scene on Saturday.

When the big day came, I holed up
in my room, salty tears welling up,
peeping at the kids' shadows
moving along the street below,
fantasizing my father's head
mashed by a meteorite, his flesh slowly
scalded by an incinerator ray-gun.

On Monday, I ran into Freddy,
stardust in his eyes. *War of the Worlds*
was scarier than he ever imagined,
the aliens' cobra-shaped heads like pissers,
protected by an impenetrable force field.

WE WERE FRIENDS

We're watching *Attack of the Giant Leeches,*
at the State Theater, M&Ms whizzing by.
You hand me Good & Plenty—my favorites—I open my mouth.

Don't eat them, you snap, *they're for throwing.*
After I'm beaned by an Atomic Fireball,
I join in pitching candy at the shadowy enemy.

When the movie ends, kids shove each other in the aisles.
Somebody yells, *I'll hop your tail.* Buck, face red,
fists balled, snarls, *Come outside and say that.*

On the sidewalk two groups face off.
I want to cut out, but you refuse to budge.
A fight breaks out. Buck socks somebody in the face.

Two others roll on the ground, streaks of blood.
I'm going home, I say. You whip off your jacket.
I don't desert my friends, you say.

SIDEKICK

I tag after Gary,
his Daisy Eagle BB gun by his side.
The grass is alive with twittering.
My parents forbid me to own a gun
and I hate them for that.
Every boy has the hunting bug
and I count on Gary letting me take a shot or two.

We enter the cool shadows of the woods,
feel the plush of pine needles underfoot,
smell the earthy dampness of decaying logs.
Gary takes aim at a Blue Jay high in a tree.
The Jay drops like a rock through the branches.
It doesn't get better than this, I tell myself,
nausea rising.

THE AWAKENING

In the 1950's, the adults of Springdale, Connecticut, mobilized to combat the growing menace posed by juvenile delinquents, aka JDs. Dressed with shirt collars up, pegged-pants down, buckle-laden black leather jackets, and motorcycle boots hiding everything from cherry bombs and whiskey nips to switchblades and knuckle-dusters—the JDs were everywhere. They took over the State Theater, where ushers were punched out, seats slashed, and smoking and heavy petting ran rampant in the back rows. Even Bill and Fred's Candy Store, just blocks from my house, turned into a hangout for sullen, spit-flicking JDs. Saint Cecilia's Church got into the act, and Father Vito, a young priest who had recently been transferred from the Bronx, regularly preached to the teens of the parish. I remember this period well because I was preparing for my confirmation, and attending Sunday mass.

I know the challenge you face, Father Vito would begin, *for it wasn't too long ago that I faced the same temptations of the flesh. How difficult it is these days to stay pure when you are besieged by dirty images in the movies, sinful language in paperback novels, and suggestive lyrics in rock 'n' roll. Now you will have a chance to know the joys of Christ, and the wholesome fun of Christian conviviality. I welcome you to experience these gifts, and more—a great spiritual awakening at our weekly Friday night Catholic Youth Organization meeting, in the church basement.*

At the first meeting, I sat nervously, scanning the room for familiar faces. I spotted Donna Vitella's backcombed bouffant hairdo and over-ripe body, imagined myself grinding with her to *In the Still of the Night*, by the Five Satins. But the sudden appearance of Father Vito's face extinguished this reverie. I also saw a few JD-types, but minus their leather jackets. Later, it was these undercover JDs who instigated a fight with some rah-rahs—super-collegiate types—and left the rest of us choking on tire smoke as they fishtailed out of the church parking lot in their chopped and channeled Mercs and souped-up Chevys.

The next week, the pastor at Saint Cecilia's, Father Kelly O'Brien, came to our second meeting and preached about *waking up to God's laws*, and remembering that since the C.Y.O. meeting was on church property, causing trouble there was *a desecration of our Lord Jesus Christ's very home*. Still, after Father O'Brien left, the JDs started another fight, stole some records, and filled the night air with the sound of blasting radios and screeching tires.

At Sunday mass before the third meeting, Father O'Brien delivered a blistering sermon, threatening to suspend the C.Y.O. if there were any further outbursts of unruly behavior. He beseeched our parents not to spare the rod when their progeny required a stern reprimand. His last words, directed at two teenage girls seated in front of him were, *Wake up to Christ, or simmer in Satan's eternal frying pan.*

The following Friday, Father Vito walked up to the microphone smiling, *I almost didn't make it here this evening—I had a close shave with my razor this morning.* After a long silence, a few forced laughs came from the front rows. I was busy staring at Donna's hefty jugs, wishing I had the nerve to ask her to dance. *Donna,* by Ritchie Valens, dominated the record charts, and I fantasized writhing with her on a couch or the back seat of a car. Father Vito was droning on about Christian rectitude, when I heard the sound of an alarm clock go off. *Trii-iing, trii-iing,* it rang, as kids snickered.

Who has the clock? Father Vito snapped.

Father Vito started to talk again. The words *wake up* died in his mouth, as a loud *trii-iing, trii-iing* echoed through the church basement.

I want that alarm clock, he yelled, heading toward the rear seats. Out of the corner of my eye, I saw a furtive passing of a big clock, with brass bells on top, under the seats towards the front rows. Father

Vito's neck bloomed red against his white collar, as he reached the back rows and couldn't find anything. He was making his way to the front when the alarm clock was passed to the back again. *Trii-iing, trii-iing,* it went, just as Father Vito reached the microphone, and was about to speak.

By now most of the kids were rolling in their seats laughing. With the exception of the JDs, who sat blankly, staring ahead, taking turns holding the clock under their seats. *Trii-iing, trii-iing,* the clock rang, as Father Vito sputtered, *Goddamn it! You're all JDs, every one of you. Get the hell out of here! Beat it! Scram! The C.Y.O. is suspended till further notice.*

Soon everyone poured out to the sidewalks, the JDs with a bopping gait to their hot rods, the cool night air electric with energy. Opening their car trunks, the JDs whipped on their glittery black leather jackets. Then, lighting up cigarettes, they slid behind their steering wheels and turned on their radios. *La Bamba,* the flip side of *Donna,* was playing, and electric guitar riffs soon drowned out our nervous laughter.

In perfect synchronization, the JDs revved up their engines. After minutes of ear-splitting pandemonium, when it sounded like their engines were about to explode, they popped their clutches, and in a crescendo of shrieking tires, covered Saint Cecilia's in an acrid cloud of smoking rubber.

CARS

THE SCAPULAR MEDAL

At fifteen, my chest was flatter than the Connecticut Thruway and lured by a Charles Atlas "Before and After" comic book ad, I bought a set of York barbells. Before my workouts, I'd kneel on my basement floor and pray for the Almighty to give me the wherewithal to build up my body to Apollonian perfection.

Soon the barbells rang out as I lifted, pushed, pulled, and after a year of working out, two hours a day, six days a week, and wolfing down soybean and fish protein powder, I packed on thirty pounds of muscle. To showcase my body, I wore a gold scapular medal around my neck that glinted in the sunlight, inscribed with four blessed images: Saint Joseph, the Virgin Mary, the Sacred Heart, and the Holy Spirit.

At Candlewood Lake, I strutted around the shoreline, dipped my hand in the water, made the sign of the cross, and dove in. I swam across the entire length of the lake and back again. Through a watery haze, I spotted some of my female classmates, who were sitting on a large log float, staring at me. Later, I fell asleep, stretched out on a white beach towel that highlighted my tan physique.

I dreamed I swam under the float where my schoolmates sat. I was about to break the surface, in a triumphant resurrection, when the chain of the scapular medal caught on a nail sticking out of a log. Try as I might to shake myself free, I ran out of breath, my lungs filled with water, and I remained lifeless, lashed to the float's bottom.

WHY DAD LOVED LOUIS ARMSTRONG

He was a guy from the gutter
who shared Dad's values: self-discipline,
self-improvement, pulling himself up
to the peak of world culture.

He could blow in a single song
250 high Cs, capped by a high F,
all played with bell-like clarity.

He grew up in the Jim Crow South
but included a white cat in his quintet.
He had a solar-powered smile
and said: *A cat is*
anybody with a good heart
who enjoys the same music together.

AT SIXTEEN

Dad gives me palm-sized monthly
calendar booklets printed by Acme
Business Consultants.
I plaster my bedroom walls
with their daily proverbs.
Words by luminaries:
Cervantes, Disraeli, Seneca;
words I copy with a flourish
of my fountain pen: "despair . . .
anxiety . . . use all wind . . . stand
begging . . . the man humbles . . .
mind . . . esteem . . . silence . . .
consent . . . audacity . . . tide turns . . .
fortune . . . fate . . . misery."

HIGH SCHOOL MOTORHEAD

Scabby knuckles from slippery wrenches

Room full of rodder mags

Life's goodies mean assorted speed options

Backseat Romeo

Start the day with a light dusting of the exterior

Hunkering down in the driver's seat

Hitting passing gear when your favorite song plays

Peeling out in front of the guys

Making the glass pack mufflers rap in front of the girls

Staying true to your car brand

SUPER SPORT, 1963

Dad said no car until I finished high school.
How I envied my classmates who drove hot rods,
gladiators revered by the guys, fawned over by the girls.

I bided my time. First I bought from the junkman
for eighty bucks, a '56 Chevy, model 210
—the lightest made—with a blown cylinder rod.

Then I bought from a guy getting married,
for five hundred dollars, a new 425 horsepower
Super Sport engine—the most potent ever made.

I covered the body with smoky gray primer,
painted in bold white letters above the right
wheel well: "THE AVENGER." And hid

both car and engine in my friend Huey's garage.
Now, my day had come to put my new Super Sport
engine into the Chevy heap of junk.

But first I had to remove the 210's broken engine.
The only kink in my plans was that, among my buddies,
only Huey had mechanical skills

and he was working that morning at the pharmacy
—where he sometimes swiped pep pills for us.
After I unbolted the old engine from its mounts,

I slid under the car to disconnect the radiator hose,
the last step before hoisting the engine from under the hood.
I just finished unscrewing the clamp, when anti-freeze

gushed in my face—I'd forgotten to drain the radiator.
I rolled from under the chassis, shrieking, sure
I'd blinded myself. I couldn't see

until Huey came and flushed out my eyes
with a garden hose. Later he gave me some pep pills
to lift my spirits.

SUBURBAN ARTICLE OF FAITH, 1961

The most beautiful girl
will put out

for the ugliest guy
if he drives a Corvette.

THE FREAK

Walt wore his sandy hair in a flattop,
studied printing at Wright Technical School,
went steady with the same girl since seventh grade.

At sixteen he got his driver's license
and, using money he inherited from an uncle,
bought a new midnight blue Chevy Impala.

Under the hood was a 283 cubic-centimeter mill—
as the rodders called their engines—with a standard
four-barrel carburetor cranking out 250 horsepower.

Nothing was modified—Walt always insisted,
and his only speed options were a Hurst four-speed
shifter and a Sun tachometer mounted on his dash.

First he was challenged by Mark, who also
drove an Impala, but with a big-block 348 cc
mill with triple deuces—three two-barrel carburetors

boasting 315 horsepower. They turned the Merritt
Parkway into a drag strip. Walt quickly pulled away
and, a mile later, was twenty car lengths ahead.

Then he took on Warren with his 390 cc
Thunderbird Special sporting dual quads—two
four-barrel Holley carbs churning out 401 horsepower.

They raced on the Connecticut Turnpike,
where Walt leaped ahead at the starting line
and won 150 dollars in a betting pool.

From then on he won race after race
against an assembly line of high-performance
Catalinas, Furies, Galaxies, and Chargers.

After every victory, Walt's girl gave him a gift:
baby booties and foam dice hung from his rear mirror,
stuffed animals lined his back window.

The hot rod set couldn't believe it, made Walt
pop his hood countless times to examine his mill.
The sight remained the same, a small-block 283

with a single four-barrel. Skeptics even tested
his gas to make sure it didn't contain jet fuel.
Then Daddy G from Portchester made the scene

in his candy-apple red Corvette Stingray
loaded with goodies like Hillborn fuel injection,
an overbored 409 cc mill with an ISKY camshaft

and Torq-thrust magnesium wheels.
He'd never lost a race. But neither had Walt,
whose car the gearheads dubbed "The Freak."

They chose Shippan Point Avenue for the showdown;
guys with walkie-talkies blocked off side streets,
looked out for police.

Five hundred dollars of bets were collected,
and after a starter's pistol was fired, Daddy G fish-tailed
off the line in a fog bank of burning rubber.

Walt stayed even with him, power shifting smoothly
into all four gears, his eyes on his tach, and beat him
at the finishing line by half a car-length.

Not long after, Walt went into the navy and his car
was never seen again. Word on the street was,
his pregnant girlfriend sank it in the Connecticut River.

MOTORHEAD'S WARDROBE

Stacked headlights
Vestigial fins
Mirror-polished valve covers
Finned air-cleaning cover
Full bubble skirts
Baseball cap headlight visor
Skull shift knob
Chrome louvered air-cleaner
Swan neck outside mirror
'53 Chevy grille teeth
Mail slot rear window
Aluminum dash knobs
Shaved door handles
Frenched taillights
Cat's-eye headlight shield

". . . the way I feel tonight." Roy Orbison

I see the squirrel's nest
rocking in the upper branches

the bleeding tiger on her back,
gunmen closing in

CLASS STRUGGLE IN THE CONNECTICUT COUNTRYSIDE

They cruise High Ridge Road,
their hopped-up Fords,
Mercs, Pontiacs, Chevys,
clumped convoy style.

With a blink of its brights,
a red MG, with shiny spoke wheels
and a foxtail streaming from its antenna
pulls up from the rear.

It weaves between one car after another
until, with a blast
of an ah-oo-gah-horn,
it cuts off the leader,
a gray chopped and channeled
'50 Ford without hubcaps.

As the MG speeds by,
the driver and passenger,
both wearing ascots and blue blazers,
laugh and flip the bird at the Ford's driver.

Above the Ford's rotting right quarter panel
is painted *Frankie's Fake-Out Wagon.*
Under the hood is a bored and stroked
350 horsepower engine with a chrome-plated
six pack—a half a dozen two-barrel carburetors.

The sucking sound of the carbs opening
acts as a signal to the other rodders,

who tromp gas pedals into a cacophony
of roaring engines and screeching tires.

In minutes the convoy catches up
to the sports car, forcing it off the road
onto a soft shoulder. Rodders pile out
and pull the blazer boys out of their car.

First, spit flies; then fists and kicks follow.
Somebody grabs a tire iron,
smashes windows, mangles the silver gauges
in the mahogany dashboard.

The Ford's driver shoves the foxtail
into the MG's exhaust pipe
before racing off, leaving a 50-foot strip
of rubber on the roadside.

STONE WALLS

Dad Was a Businessman

and his solution to anything I asked was:
It's whatever the market will bear.

Why are prisons filled with colored people?
Why have presidents only been men?
Why are the Marines in Laos and Panama?
Why are people eating out of garbage cans?
Why do we have 70,000 nuclear warheads?
Why do people die in emergency rooms
waiting to be seen by a doctor?

It's whatever the market will bear.

STONE WALLS

People say it's in Dad's blood
—an Italian thing—his ability to place
each stone precisely where it belongs.

Dad's proud of his work. He lets me
hand him rocks, but he's the only one allowed
to use hammer and chisel to shape and fit them.

He's a neatnik and his basement workbench
has every manner of gadget and tool,
though he doesn't show me how to use them.

I struggle to saw, hammer, and screw together
a wooden cage for my pet serpents.
Most escape through the chicken-wire mesh.

When I say I'd rather play with my friends
than work in the yard, Dad repeats: *A man
either earns his bread with his brain or his back.*

Mom finds a snake in the kitchen,
and says she's going to crown me.
I love to read; maybe I'll try my brain.

GUIDER'S FIELD

I craved Big John Cerelli's daughter, Connie,
and looked for any excuse to hang around her house.
One day I showed her some blue cardboard folders
that held my coin collection,
when Big John asked to see them.

While he sat on his front porch
looking at my coin folders,
I whispered to Connie I loved her lips,
her shapely figure, the way her hair bounced
on her shoulders.
When Big John returned my coin books,
I noticed an Indian Head penny
missing, but I didn't say anything.

The next day I came with more folders
and again Big John asked to see them,
and I whispered to Connie
she looked good, smelled good,
squeezed her hand and asked her
to walk with me through Guider's Field,
a place where we could lie down
and nobody could see us. There were a million
things I wanted to say and do.
Later Big John gave back my folders,
and I noticed there was a Flying Eagle
quarter missing, but I didn't say anything.

The next day I let Big John
look at my coin folders, and instead
of Connie coming out of her house,
her mother came out and said Connie
was a decent girl who deserved to be
respected and I shouldn't forget it.
Then she went inside and I saw Connie
staring at me from her bedroom window.

When Big John gave back my folders,
I noticed two Standing Liberty half dollars
were missing. Again I didn't say
anything and, after he left, I stepped over
the stone wall in front of Guider's field,
and, kicking stones along a cow path,
watched the green spears of wheat
quiver in the breeze.

"HELLO STRANGER" BY BARBARA LEWIS

Shadow of a brook trout in still water
Odor of rotting toadstools
Drizzle brightens the yellow lichen

SHAME

Fishing
in the backwater
I pull from the bottom
a grayish lump of life
glistening like semen
with no eyes
and wiry whiskers.
Hearing it croak
I run to show my father
hiding behind a hedge
of swamp grass.

HANGING OUT WITH RICHIE

I'm at Brewster Lanes,
eyeing Richie clean his teeth
with a matchbook cover.
Now and then we turn our heads
at the crashing of balls and pins
checking out if any chicks
have come through the door.

I'm on winter break, rattling on
how much I hate the cadet corps
at Pennsylvania Military College:
early rising, no girls, inspections, drills.

Richie pumps gas at a Chevron Station.
He's bitching about his boss,
a real meathead, who's making him
work on Christmas. He's thinking of
joining the navy; none of the guys
are around anymore and all
the stray girls are bow wows.

I look at Richie's played-out
pompadour, his pimply mug,
the matchbook he's sawing
back and forth in his teeth.
The bartender yawns. The place
stinks of piss, stale cigarette smoke.

Richie sits up, points to the TV
at a Gina Lollabrigida look-alike.

I'd hump her till she has a heart attack,
his eyes growing larger, looking down
at the brown stump of a tooth
rolling between his fingers.

MURRAY THE K'S 1964 HOLIDAY REVUE

Below the marquee
of the Brooklyn Fox Theater,
police on horseback fight to keep surging fans
from flooding Flatbush Avenue.

Yolk-yellow bulbs bathe the names in light:
Smokey Robinson and the Miracles, the Marvelettes,
Screaming Jay Hawkins, Chuck Jackson,
Dionne Warwick, Mary Wells, the Shangri-Las.

Wooden barricades fall,
teens storm through brass doors,
charging down aisles smelling of Dixie Peach,
Acqua Net, Wildroot Cream Oil.

Near the stage, a holdout from an earlier show
refuses to budge from her seat.
A uniformed guard twice her size pulls on her arm,
leveraging his big butt to raise her skinny one,
never expecting the uppercut to his jaw.

Later Murray shimmies into the lights
with his arms around Dionne,
Chuck throws first his tie,
then his jacket, to his fans,
the crowd roars, *Do the Monkey!* to the Miracles'
choreographed mugging,
and Screaming Jay shrieks, *I'm Gonna Put a Spell on You!*

RACE RELATIONS

Mom and Dad bickered
about who best represented
the Negro race.
Dad loved Louis Armstrong,
Nat King Cole, Sammy Davis, Jr.
Mom favored Martin Luther King,
Harry Belafonte, Rosa Parks.

Dad took me to an exhibition game
of the Harlem Globetrotters
at Boyle Stadium when I started
going to Stamford High School.
Natural ball players, he said,
shaking some licorice nibs
from a yellow packet.
*Colored people can do more
than play basketball,* I said,
biting hard on the licorice.
I didn't say . . . dad stammered.
You didn't have to . . . I hammered.
It was the start of a long season.

In time, Dad quit talking to the ticket
collector on his commuter train
after the trainman called Johnny Mathis
a nigger fag. I fell out with Mom
when she trashed me for touting
Malcolm X and Eldridge Cleaver
and wearing a white tee shirt

with a black hand on an AK47
that read *By Any Means Necessary.*

"DRIP DROP" BY DION

A shutter slaps against the side of a barn
A hornet's nest falls on a litter of piglets
Nurses stab a surgeon with wooden tongue depressors
A thousand bowling balls stream across an airport runway

FACTORY JOB, 1969

Greenwich, Connecticut

Clean white face with dirty drug habit, I work as an inspector in a Timex assembly plant. Immigrant faces: Jamaican, Puerto Rican, Italian, peg away at plastic display cases; gluing, screwing, cringing, as bad-ass black straw boss—who plays golf with the real white boss—ladles out insults and limits bathroom breaks to three minutes. At lunchtime I swipe a handbag, hit the shithouse (my visits go unnoticed), rifle through rosary beads, pennies, pay stubs, lottery tickets, green card. I plunge back into work-floor chaos, as straw boss next to the real boss slams workers for being a bunch of thievin' motherfuckers.

I MEET DAD HIGH ON HEROIN

at the information booth
with the four-faced clock
at Grand Central station.

He's fifty-seven, at the top
of his corporate game: promotion
to Director, foxy secretary,
executive suite office
in the Empire State Building.

Dad pays for my train ticket;
we sleep all the way to Stamford.
Exiting the commuter parking lot,
he eyes me, *You don't look right.*
It's hay fever season, I mumble,
cigarette singeing his suit jacket.

BUGHOUSE BIRTHDAY

Days before I turned 24,
I told my family doctor
I had a heroin habit
and, blinking like a mosquito landed
in his eye, he sent me to an upstate
loony bin.

There was no group therapy,
no individual sessions,
no psycho-education,
no 12-step programs.
The attendants communicated
with grunts and hand gestures
behind shatterproof glass.
When I complained of withdrawal symptoms,
the nurse said junkies
have a low threshold for pain.

A patient who memorized
Edgar Allan Poe
kept me up nights ranting:
"Ghastly grin and ancient raven
wandering from the nightly shore. . ."
Another called me paesan'
and said a Mafia hit team
was out gunning for him,
smashing the TV against a wall,
inches above my head.

My roomies boasted
how they played the skull doctors
by faking psychiatric problems
to avoid jail time,
fantasizing out loud how much
dope they were going to shoot
the minute they hit the streets.

When I was discharged,
they gave me the phone numbers
to their connections.

Sobered by my hospital stay,
I stuck to wine coolers and reefer
for three months.

ADMISSIONS

That evening we rode in silence
until we reached the iron gates

of Fairfield Hills State Hospital,
when Dad's face crumpled

into the steering wheel and a sob
shook tears on his marble cheeks.

THE REFUSENIK

When Dad worked as a purchasing agent,
he recalled how salesmen
offered him bribes: cash,
Broadway theater tickets,
vacations in the Caribbean,
in exchange for their business.
I told people I admired him
for his integrity,
but inside a voice sneered:
square, dope, for refusing
whatever perks came his way.

Once, while returning from lunch,
a pipe dropped from a skyscraper,
grazing Dad's forehead.
He struggled to stay conscious,
while colleagues led him to a doctor,
who said he was lucky to be alive
and urged him to seek legal counsel.

My father refused,
saying it was wrong to sue
for damages when he wasn't
really hurt. I shrugged my shoulders,
but inside a voice hissed: fool,
goody-goody; who in their right mind
turns down free money.

Years later I sat in a car with friends,
green in the gills on Gallo Port
and bogus Acapulco Gold,
when a tow truck ran a red light
and plowed into our passenger side.
The driver sat dazed
while I tumbled out the crumpled door
and stuffed wine bottles and a hash pipe
down a sewer drain.

We found an attorney
fresh out of law school
who said a lack of injuries
never stood in the way
of a big payday, and sent us
to orthopedists and surgeons
who never treated us.
We each made 700 bucks.

A year later, I used my money
to buy my girlfriend a ruby-cluster
heart ring for Valentine's Day
while I was rehabilitating
in a drug program my father
refused to visit.

THE NEW JACKET

After my ex kicked me out and kept me from living with my son, I brought him with me on the weekends to my parents' house in Connecticut. Filled with hurt, I found comfort in the trees, lawns, quiet roads winding through Stamford, where I grew up.

One weekend, I picked up my son and took an immediate dislike to his new jacket when he told me his mom bought it. It stank like foam rubber and I remember thinking—what a phony piece of crap— a brown plastic bag passing as a leather jacket. There was no end to the cheap tricks my ex would pull to buy his affection.

A natural athlete, my son had a great sense of balance and, ignoring his concerns about his new jacket—of which he was eleven year-old proud—I persuaded him to go down a steep hill; standing on his skateboard. His long lashes trembled as he soared down the hill, falling, sliding across the asphalt, shearing off the top buttons of his jacket, and scraping deep rut marks into its soft finish. When I helped him up, he gave me a look that said: *Why did you do that, Dad? Why did you make me ruin my new leather jacket?*

DOO WOP ORNITHOLOGY

Quails
    Blue Jays
        Larks
            Sparrows
                Parakeets
                    Pelicans
                        Penguins
                            Crows
                                Orioles
                                    Swallows
                                  Wrens
                            Ravens
                        Robins
                  Falcons
              Flamingos
            Ospreys
          Cardinals
      Hawks
Starlings

Stone Walls — 103 — Fagiani

THE CINDER BLOCK WALL

On a sunny October day in 1950, my parents moved from an apartment in the Italian neighborhood of Villa Avenue in the Bronx to a modest Cape Cod house in Springdale, Connecticut. Like thousands of veterans of World War II, my father took advantage of the GI Bill to secure a 30-year mortgage on a house that sold for $12,000 dollars. The area surrounding our new suburban community —the Colony, as my father called it— remained largely undeveloped, and a brook trickled along the side of our house, fed by two cement pipes that carried water under an adjacent intersection. Four years later, following a heavy downpour, the pipes couldn't handle the increased water volume and the brook overflowed pouring across the intersection, flooding our front yard.

My father built a cinder block wall around the perimeter of our property, a bulwark in the event the brook overflowed in the future. He made it sturdy, so the foundation rested on a cement base more than a foot underground, but also artfully, so it had a serrated look, and all the rough surfaces were capped with smooth, white cement. It stood out among the green lawns and white picket fences of Connecticut. One of our Yankee neighbors commented on the Italian obsession with mortar and building block.

From August 11 to August 12, 1955, Hurricane Connie dropped 6 inches of rain on Southern Connecticut, while less than a week later, Hurricane Diane dumped another 20 inches of water. Flooding was immediate and devastating. The New Haven Railroad lost 10 bridges, 100 people died—including some in Springdale—and the damage, by today's standards, was $4 billion. The sky stayed black for days and the rain never let up. The meandering brook next to our house turned into a raging river; uprooted trees and rumbling boulders swept up in its current kept me awake. A Statewide emergency was declared, the National Guard mobilized, and we had to abandon our home to stay with hilltop neighbors.

That night we left, I stepped out the front door, only to see how the street had transformed into a river that swept across our neighbors' property and emptied into what had been our brook. I waded through the waist-high water clutching my mother's hand, terrified the current tugging at my legs would sweep me into the cauldron of churning water further ahead. As I walked, I saw my father in a frenzy of motion, his face shrouded in a floppy rain hat, piling burlap bags filled with sand on top of his cinder block wall, inundated on all sides by water.

When the rain stopped, we returned. All around our house were cavernous craters, piles of stones and debris left in the wake of the storm. The water had risen in our next-door neighbor's basement until it flooded out their living room. Indeed, every house in the Colony suffered water damage as a result of basement flooding. Our house was the one exception. The interior remained completely unscathed by Diane's destruction.

Nearly sixty years later, and long after my father's demise from a heart attack, I occasionally walk past the house where I grew up in Connecticut. Its most recent owners have converted the modest Cape Cod into a hideous barracks-like structure, but the cinder block wall still stands.

CHIPPIES

On holidays, my Aunt Tosca,
named after the opera,
gave her brother Mario,
named after the opera's hero,
a jar of reddish onions
called *ci-pol-li-ni*.

They swam in vinegar
like pickled fingertips,
biting and sour.
People would make faces
and say *how could
anybody eat those things,*
as Mario, my father,
crunched them in his mouth.

In time, macaroni became *macs*
spaghetti became *spags*
and *cipollini* became *chippies*.
And the day came
when my father told Tosca
his plumbing could no longer take
those spicy bombs from the Old World.

At my Aunt Tosca's wake,
long after my father's death,
no opera music is playing.
I look at the handful of relatives
and wonder who has the goodness
to give *cipollini*
and who has the fire to devour them?

MUSICAL SOURCES

1. "So Rare," Jimmy Dorsey.
2. "The Howdy Doody Show Theme," Buffalo Bob Smith.
3. "Rumble," Link Ray.
4. "Don't Let Go," Roy Hamilton.
5. "We Belong Together," Robert & Johnny.
6. "In the Still of the Night," Five Satins.
7. "Donna," Ritchie Valens.
8. "La Bamba," Ritchie Valens.
9. "Hello Stranger," Barbara Lewis.
10. "Stormy Weather," The Spaniels.
11. "What Time Is It," The Jive Five.
12. "The Ten Commandments of Love," Harvey and the Moonglows.
13. "Green Onions, Booker T. & the MGs.
14. "Mack the Knife," Louis Armstrong.
15. "409," The Beach Boys.
16. "Only the Lonely," Roy Orbison.
17. "Drip Drop," Dion DiMucci.
18. "Rock Around the Clock," Bill Haley and the Comets.
19. "Mickey's Monkey," Smokey Robinson and the Miracles.
20. "Strange I Know," Marvelettes.
21. "Any Day Now," Chuck Jackson.
22. "Laughing Boy," Mary Wells.
23. "Leader of the Pack," Shangri-Las.
24. "I'm Gonna Put a Spell On You," Screaming Jay Hawkins.
25. "Memories Are Made of This," Dean Martin.
26. "Nature Boy," Nat King Cole.
27. "The Candy Man," Sammy Davis Jr.
28. "Matilda," Harry Belafonte.
29. "Misty," Johnny Mathis.
30. "Celeste Aida," Enrico Caruso.

31 "Locomotion," Lilttle Eva.
32 "He's a Rebel," The Crystals.
33 "I Get Around," The Beach Boys."

AUTHOR'S NOTE

GIL FAGIANI is an independent scholar, translator, essayist, short story writer, and poet. His translations have appeared in such anthologies as *A New Map: The Poetry of Migrant Writers in Italy,* edited by Mia Lecomte and Luigi Bonaffini; *Poets of the Italian Diaspora,* edited by Luigi Bonaffini and Joseph Perricone; and *Italoamericana: The Literature of the Great Migration, 1880-1943,* edited by Francesco Durante and Robert Viscusi (American Edition).

His first poetry collection *Rooks,* is set at Pennsylvania Military College in the 1960s, (Rain Mountain Press, 2007); *A Blanquito in El Barrio* (Rain Mountain Press, 2009) pulses with the streets and music of Spanish Harlem; *Chianti in Connecticut* (Bordighera Press, 2010) focuses on the immigrant generation of his family, as well as his childhood in Stamford, Connecticut; and *Serfs of Psychiatry* (Finishing Line Press, 2012) was inspired by his experience working in a state psychiatric hospital for twelve years.

Fagiani is a founder and host of the Third Friday Queens Writers reading series in Astoria, New York City, co-curates the Italian American Writers' Association's reading series, and is an associate editor of *Feile-Festa: A Literary Arts Journal*. A social worker and addiction specialist by profession, Fagiani directed a residential treatment program for recovering alcoholics and drug addicts in downtown Brooklyn for 21 years. Earlier this year, he was the subject of a *New York Times* article by David Gonzalez, "A Poet Mines Memories of Drug Addiction."

VIA FOLIOS
A refereed book series dedicated to the culture of Italians and Italian Americans.

LOUISE DESALVO. *Casting Off.* Vol 100 Fiction. $22
MARY JO BONA. *I stop waiting for You.* Vol 99 Poetry. $12
RACHEL GUIDO DEVRIES. *Stati zitt, Josie.* Vol 98 Children's Literature. $8
GRACE CAVALIERI. *The Mandate of Heaven.* Vol 97 Poetry. $14
MARISA FRASCA. *Via incanto.* Vol 96 Poetry. $12
DOUGLAS GLADSTONE. *Carving a Niche for Himself.* Vol 95 History. $12
MARIA TERRONE. *Eye to Eye.* Vol 94 Poetry. $14
CONSTANCE SANCETTA. *Here in Cerchio* Vol 93 Local History. $15
MARIA MAZZIOTTI GILLAN. *Ancestors' Song* Vol 92 Poetry. $14
DARRELL FUSARO. *What if Godzilla Just Wanted a Hug?* Vol ? Essays. $TBA
MICHAEL PARENTI. *Waiting for Yesterday: Pages from a Street Kid's Life.* Vol 90 Memoir. $15
ANNIE LANZILOTTO, *Schistsong*, Vol. 89. Poetry, $15
EMANUEL DI PASQUALE, *Love Lines*, Vol. 88. Poetry, $10
CAROSONE & LOGIUDICE. *Our Naked Lives.* Vol 87 Essays. $15
JAMES PERICONI. *Strangers in a Strange Land: A Survey of Italian-Language American Books.* Vol. 86. Book History. $24
DANIELA GIOSEFFI, *Escaping La Vita Della Cucina*, Vol. 85. Essays & Creative Writing. $22
MARIA FAMÀ, *Mystics in the Family*, Vol. 84. Poetry, $10
ROSSANA DEL ZIO, *From Bread and Tomatoes to Zuppa di Pesce "Ciambotto"*, Vol. 83. $15
LORENZO DELBOCA, *Polentoni*, Vol. 82. Italian Studies, $15
SAMUEL GHELLI, *A Reference Grammar*, Vol. 81. Italian Language. $36
ROSS TALARICO, *Sled Run*, Vol. 80. Fiction. $15
FRED MISURELLA, *Only Sons*, Vol. 79. Fiction. $14
FRANK LENTRICCHIA, *The Portable Lentricchia*, Vol. 78. Fiction. $16
RICHARD VETERE, *The Other Colors in a Snow Storm*, Vol. 77. Poetry. $10
GARIBALDI LAPOLLA, *Fire in the Flesh*, Vol. 76 Fiction & Criticism. $25
GEORGE GUIDA, *The Pope Stories*, Vol. 75 Prose. $15
ROBERT VISCUSI, *Ellis Island*, Vol. 74. Poetry. $28
ELENA GIANINI BELOTTI, *The Bitter Taste of Strangers Bread*, Vol. 73, Fiction, $24
PINO APRILE, *Terroni*, Vol. 72, Italian Studies, $20
EMANUEL DI PASQUALE, *Harvest*, Vol. 71, Poetry, $10
ROBERT ZWEIG, *Return to Naples*, Vol. 70, Memoir, $16
AIROS & CAPPELLI, *Guido*, Vol. 69, Italian/American Studies, $12
FRED GARDAPHÉ, *Moustache Pete is Dead! Long Live Moustache Pete!*, Vol. 67, Literature/Oral History, $12
PAOLO RUFFILLI, *Dark Room/Camera oscura*, Vol. 66, Poetry, $11
HELEN BAROLINI, *Crossing the Alps*, Vol. 65, Fiction, $14
COSMO FERRARA, *Profiles of Italian Americans*, Vol. 64, Italian Americana, $16
GIL FAGIANI, *Chianti in Connecticut*, Vol. 63, Poetry, $10
BASSETTI & D'ACQUINO, *Italic Lessons*, Vol. 62, Italian/American Studies, $10
CAVALIERI & PASCARELLI, Eds., *The Poet's Cookbook*, Vol. 61, Poetry/Recipes, $12
EMANUEL DI PASQUALE, *Siciliana*, Vol. 60, Poetry, $8
NATALIA COSTA, Ed., *Bufalini*, Vol. 59, Poetry. $18.
RICHARD VETERE, *Baroque*, Vol. 58, Fiction. $18.

Bordighera Press is an imprint of Bordighera, Incorporated, an independently owned not-for-profit scholarly organization that has no legal affiliation with the University of Central Florida or with The John D. Calandra Italian American Institute, Queens College/CUNY.

LEWIS TURCO, *La Famiglia/The Family*, Vol. 57, Memoir, $15
NICK JAMES MILETI, *The Unscrupulous*, Vol. 56, Humanities, $20
BASSETTI, ACCOLLA, D'AQUINO, *Italici: An Encounter with Piero Bassetti*, Vol. 55, Italian Studies, $8
GIOSE RIMANELLI, *The Three-legged One*, Vol. 54, Fiction, $15
CHARLES KLOPP, *Bele Antiche Stòrie*, Vol. 53, Criticism, $25
JOSEPH RICAPITO, *Second Wave*, Vol. 52, Poetry, $12
GARY MORMINO, *Italians in Florida*, Vol. 51, History, $15
GIANFRANCO ANGELUCCI, *Federico F.*, Vol. 50, Fiction, $15
ANTHONY VALERIO, *The Little Sailor*, Vol. 49, Memoir, $9
ROSS TALARICO, *The Reptilian Interludes*, Vol. 48, Poetry, $15
RACHEL GUIDO DE VRIES, *Teeny Tiny Tino's Fishing Story*, Vol. 47, Children's Literature, $6
EMANUEL DI PASQUALE, *Writing Anew*, Vol. 46, Poetry, $15
MARIA FAMÀ, *Looking For Cover*, Vol. 45, Poetry, $12
ANTHONY VALERIO, *Toni Cade Bambara's One Sicilian Night*, Vol. 44, Poetry, $10
EMANUEL CARNEVALI, Dennis Barone, Ed., *Furnished Rooms*, Vol. 43, Poetry, $14
BRENT ADKINS, et al., Ed., *Shifting Borders, Negotiating Places*, Vol. 42, Proceedings, $18
GEORGE GUIDA, *Low Italian*, Vol. 41, Poetry, $11
GARDAPHÈ, GIORDANO, TAMBURRI, *Introducing Italian Americana*, Vol. 40, Italian/American Studies, $10
DANIELA GIOSEFFI, *Blood Autumn/Autunno di sangue*, Vol. 39, Poetry, $15/$25
FRED MISURELLA, *Lies to Live by*, Vol. 38, Stories, $15
STEVEN BELLUSCIO, *Constructing a Bibliography*, Vol. 37, Italian Americana, $15
ANTHONY JULIAN TAMBURRI, Ed., *Italian Cultural Studies 2002*, Vol. 36, Essays, $18
BEA TUSIANI, *con amore*, Vol. 35, Memoir, $19
FLAVIA BRIZIO-SKOV, Ed., *Reconstructing Societies in the Aftermath of War*, Vol. 34, History, $30
TAMBURRI, et al., Eds., *Italian Cultural Studies 2001*, Vol. 33, Essays, $18
ELIZABETH G. MESSINA, Ed., *In Our Own Voices*, Vol. 32, Italian/American Studies, $25
STANISLAO G. PUGLIESE, *Desperate Inscriptions*, Vol. 31, History, $12
HOSTERT & TAMBURRI, Eds., *Screening Ethnicity*, Vol. 30, Italian/American Culture, $25
G. PARATI & B. LAWTON, Eds., *Italian Cultural Studies*, Vol. 29, Essays, $18
HELEN BAROLINI, *More Italian Hours*, Vol. 28, Fiction, $16
FRANCO NASI, Ed., *Intorno alla Via Emilia*, Vol. 27, Culture, $16
ARTHUR L. CLEMENTS, *The Book of Madness & Love*, Vol. 26, Poetry, $10
JOHN CASEY, et al., *Imagining Humanity*, Vol. 25, Interdisciplinary Studies, $18
ROBERT LIMA, *Sardinia/Sardegna*, Vol. 24, Poetry, $10
DANIELA GIOSEFFI, *Going On*, Vol. 23, Poetry, $10
ROSS TALARICO, *The Journey Home*, Vol. 22, Poetry, $12
EMANUEL DI PASQUALE, *The Silver Lake Love Poems*, Vol. 21, Poetry, $7
JOSEPH TUSIANI, *Ethnicity*, Vol. 20, Poetry, $12
JENNIFER LAGIER, *Second Class Citizen*, Vol. 19, Poetry, $8
FELIX STEFANILE, *The Country of Absence*, Vol. 18, Poetry, $9
PHILIP CANNISTRARO, *Blackshirts*, Vol. 17, History, $12
LUIGI RUSTICHELLI, Ed., *Seminario sul racconto*, Vol. 16, Narrative, $10
LEWIS TURCO, *Shaking the Family Tree*, Vol. 15, Memoirs, $9
LUIGI RUSTICHELLI, Ed., *Seminario sulla drammaturgia*, Vol. 14, Theater/Essays, $10
FRED GARDAPHÈ, *Moustache Pete is Dead! Long Live Moustache Pete!*, Vol. 13, Oral Literature, $10
JONE GAILLARD CORSI, *Il libretto d'autore*, 1860–1930, Vol. 12, Criticism, $17
HELEN BAROLINI, *Chiaroscuro: Essays of Identity*, Vol. 11, Essays, $15
PICARAZZI & FEINSTEIN, Eds., *An African Harlequin in Milan*, Vol. 10, Theater/Essays, $15

JOSEPH RICAPITO, *Florentine Streets & Other Poems*, Vol. 9, Poetry, $9

FRED MISURELLA, *Short Time*, Vol. 8, Novella, $7

NED CONDINI, *Quartettsatz*, Vol. 7, Poetry, $7

ANTHONY JULIAN TAMBURRI, Ed., *Fuori: Essays by Italian/American Lesbians and Gays*, Vol. 6, Essays, $10

ANTONIO GRAMSCI, P. Verdicchio, Trans. & Intro. , *The Southern Question*, Vol. 5, Social Criticism, $5

DANIELA GIOSEFFI, *Word Wounds & Water Flowers*, Vol. 4, Poetry, $8

WILEY FEINSTEIN, *Humility's Deceit: Calvino Reading Ariosto Reading Calvino*, Vol. 3, Criticism, $10

PAOLO A. GIORDANO, Ed., *Joseph Tusiani: Poet, Translator, Humanist*, Vol. 2, Criticism, $25

ROBERT VISCUSI, *Oration Upon the Most Recent Death of Christopher Columbus*, Vol. 1, Poetry, $3

www.ingramcontent.com/pod-product-compliance
Lightning Source LLC
LaVergne TN
LVHW041259080426
835510LV00009B/805